ECK THE HALL

SOLO CELLO

Traditional Welsh Carol
Arranged by BRUCE HEALEY

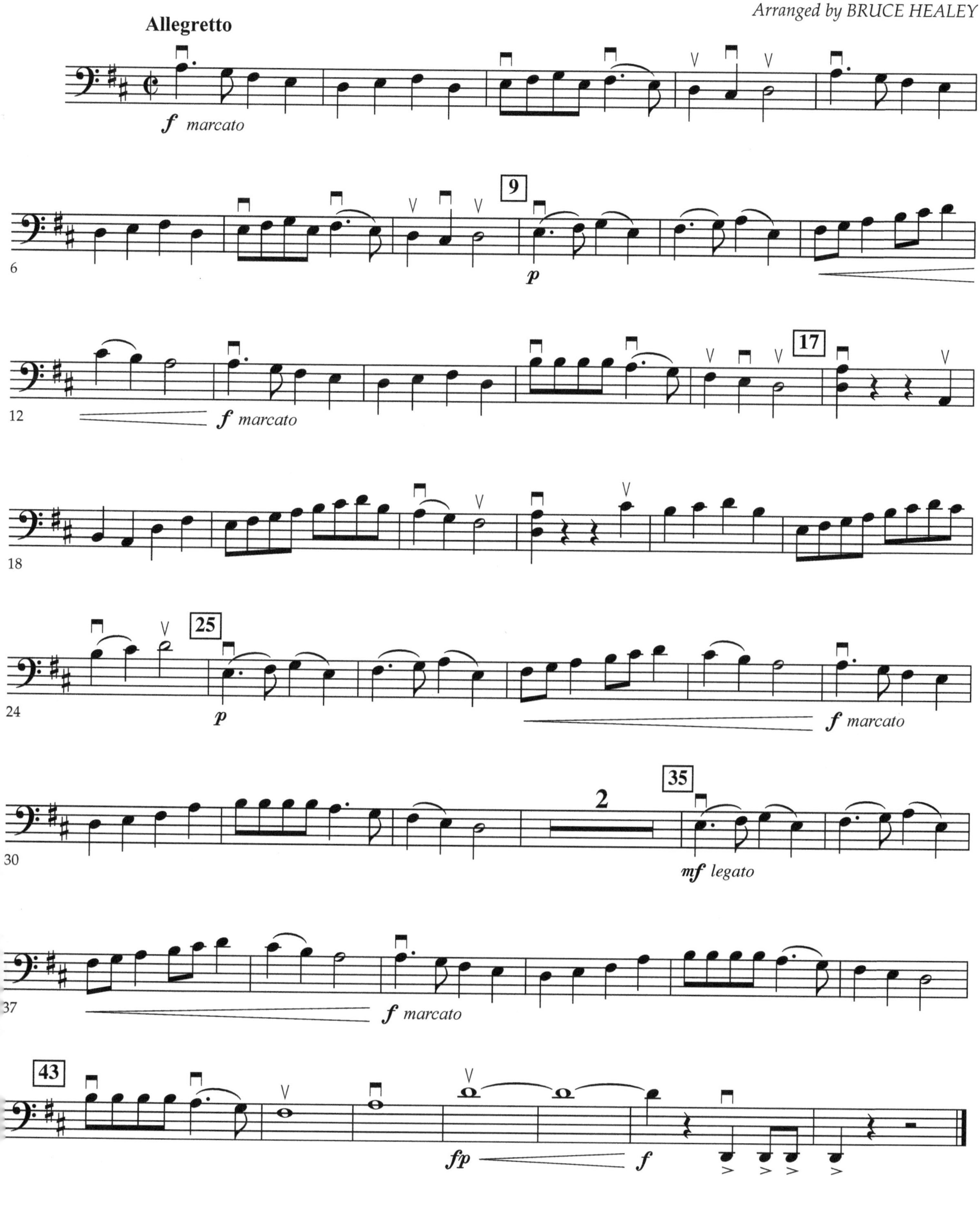

0842195

AWAY IN A MANGER

SOLO CELLO

Words by JOHN T. McFARLAND (v.3)
Music by JAMES R. MURRAY
Arranged by BRUCE HEALEY

00842195

GREENSLEEVES

SOLO CELLO

16th Century Traditional English
Arranged by BRUCE HEALEY

GOD REST YE MERRY, GENTLEMEN

SOLO CELLO

19th Century English Carol
Arranged by BRUCE HEALEY

00842195

O COME, ALL YE FAITHFUL
(Adeste Fideles)

SOLO CELLO

Music by JOHN FRANCIS WADE
Latin Words translated by FREDERICK OAKELEY
Arranged by BRUCE HEALEY

SILENT NIGHT

7

SOLO CELLO

Words by JOSEPH MOHR
Translated by JOHN F. YOUNG
Music by FRANZ X. GRUBER
Arranged by BRUCE HEALEY

00842195

DING DONG! MERRILY ON HIGH!

SOLO CELLO

French Carol
Arranged by BRUCE HEALEY

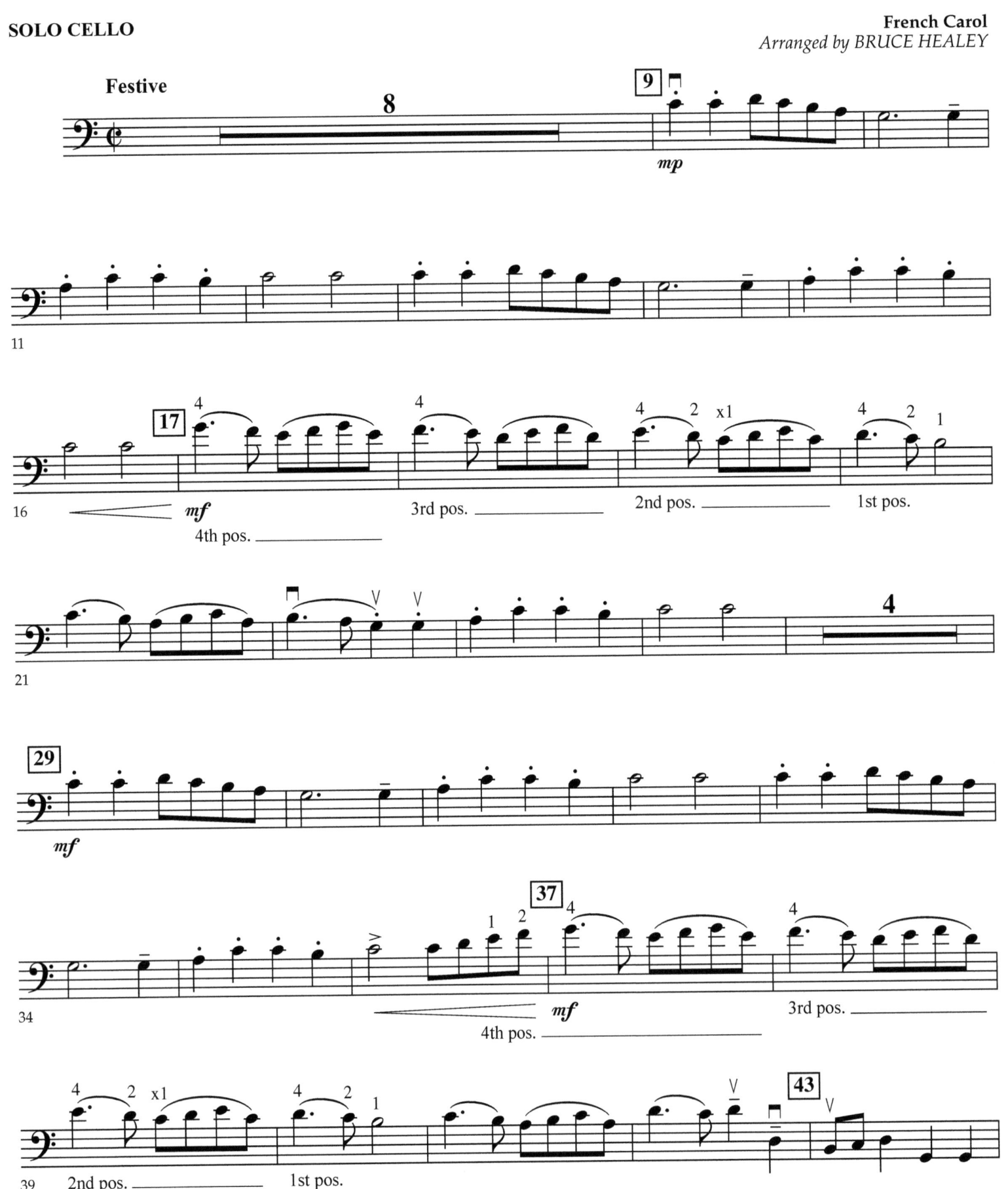

CHANUKAH, OY CHANUKAH

SOLO CELLO

Traditional Hebrew Lyrics
Chanukah Melody
Arranged by BRUCE HEALEY

35
40
45
4th pos.
3rd pos.
4th pos.
3rd pos.
49
1st pos.
53
55
mp cresc.
58
62
p cresc.
3rd pos.
1st pos.
2nd pos.

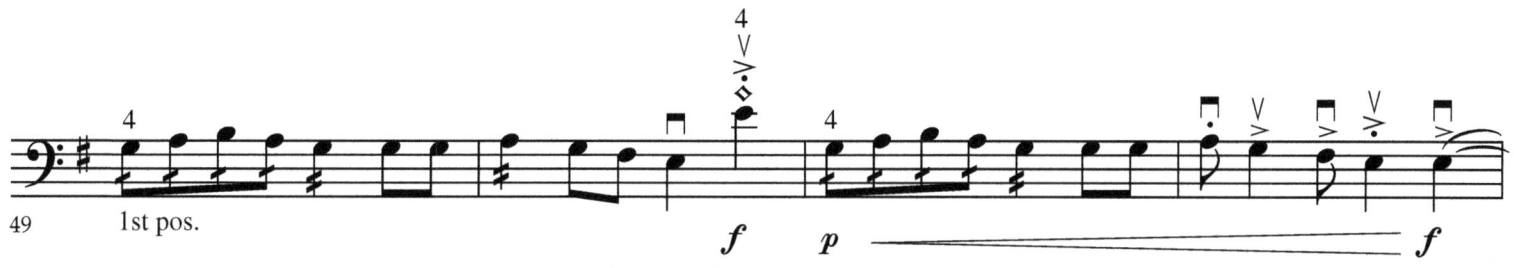

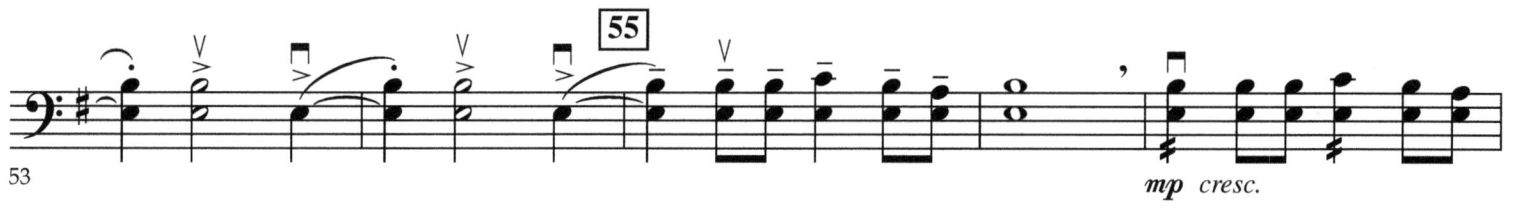

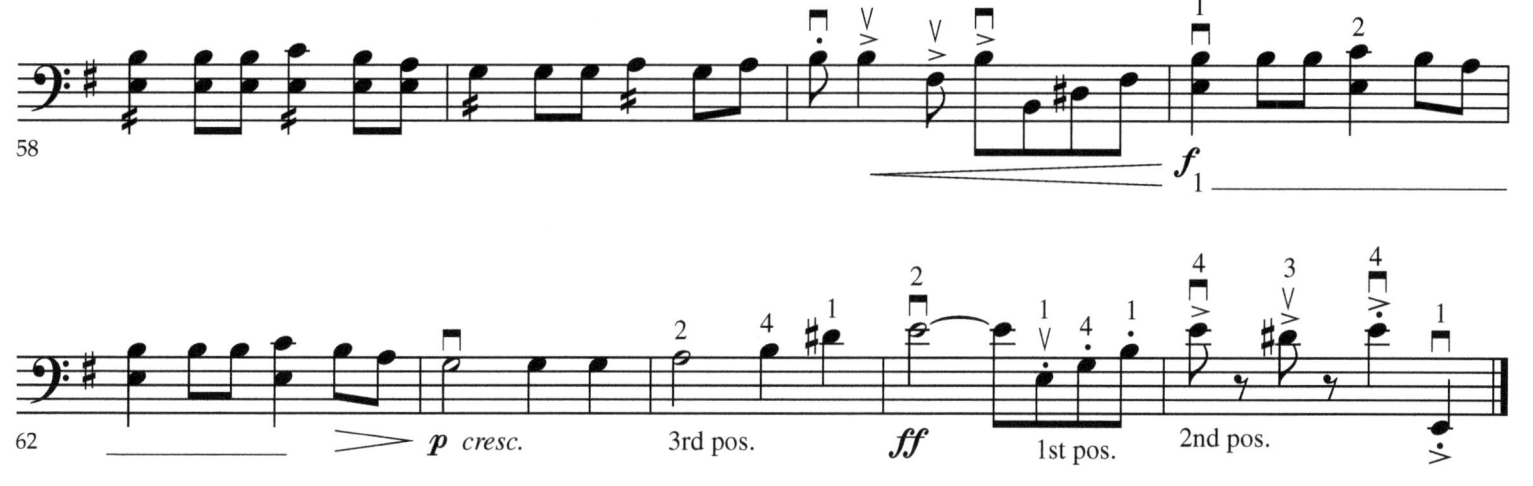

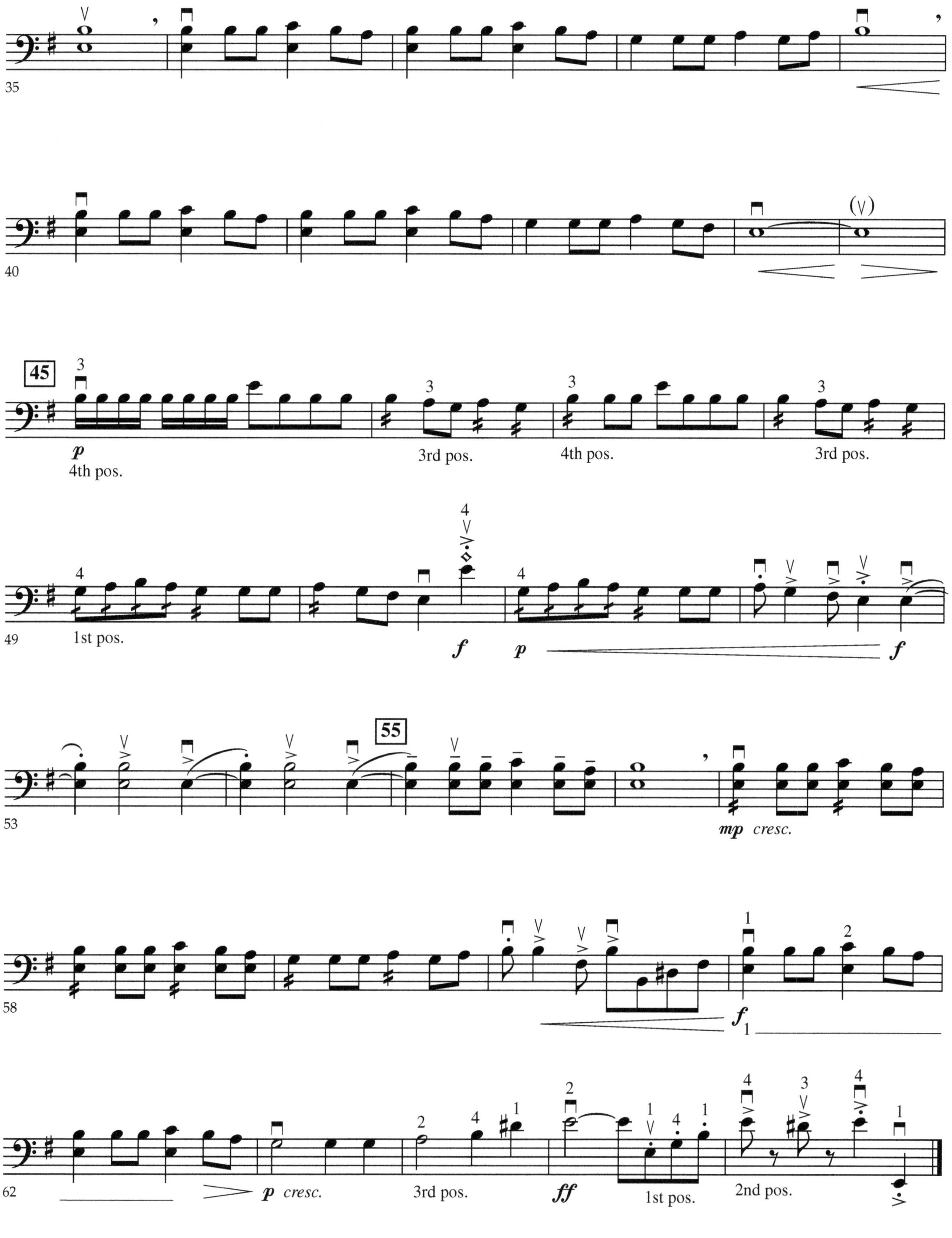

12

PAT-A-PAN
(Willie, Take Your Little Drum)

SOLO CELLO

Words and Music by BERNARD de la MONNOYE
Arranged by BRUCE HEALEY

00842195

O HOLY NIGHT

SOLO CELLO

French Words by PLACIDE CAPPEAU
English Words by JOHN S. DWIGHT
Music by ADOLPHE ADAM
Arranged by BRUCE HEALEY

THREE HOLIDAY SONGS
(The Dreydl Song • Jingle Bells • Joy To The World)

SOLO CELLO

Arranged by BRUCE HEALEY

"Joy To The World"
Words by ISAAC WATTS
Music by GEORGE FRIDERIC HANDEL

WE WISH YOU A MERRY CHRISTMAS

SOLO CELLO

Traditional English Folksong
Arranged by BRUCE HEALEY